The

Understanding Weather Just for Kids!

KidCaps is An Imprint of BookCaps™

www.bookcaps.com

© 2013. All Rights Reserved.

Table of Contents

ABOUT KIDCAPS..4

INTRODUCTION 5

CHAPTER 1: WHAT IS A TSUNAMI?..9
    Waves...18

CHAPTER 2: SCIENCE OF TSUNAMI'S 24
    Causes 26
        Plate Tectonics/Earthquakes 27
        Landslides 31
        Volcanoes..34
        Meteorites 37

CHAPTER 3: WHERE TSUNAMIS STRIKE 40
    Development...44
    Kinds of Tsunamis—Distant and Local 48
    Prediction...51

CHAPTER 4: WARNING SIGNS 58
    Warning Systems 63

CHAPTER 5:RICHTER SCALE 69
    Damage 71
    Cleaning Up 75

CHAPTER 6: FAMOUS TSUNAMIS 78
    8 Deadliest Tsunamis..78
    Notable Tsunamis in History 79

CHAPTER 7: STUDYING 87
    Safety 89

CONCLUSION 91

BIBLIOGRAPHY..91

About KidCaps

KidCaps is an imprint of BookCaps™ that is just for kids! Each month BookCaps will be releasing several books in this exciting imprint. Visit are website or like us on Facebook to see more!

Introduction

While the sea brings life and livelihood to many people in the world, it can also bring unexpected disaster and destruction. Every year, Tsunamis strike. Every year, they bring devastation in their wake.

Tsunamis are powerful waves in the ocean that carry a massive destructive force. Tsunamis can snap trees in two, destroy houses, and toss ships and boats onto shore. They will wipe out everything in their path and flood large areas of land that is at a low level.

Tsunamis have been around for as long as humans have existed. Scientists and geologists have found evidence that reveals tsunamis have occurred worldwide throughout the history of the earth. Today, people living on islands in the Pacific, such as Hawaii, are most in danger of experiencing a tsunami.

The good news is that tsunamis do not occur particularly often. As few as five tsunamis are recorded every year, and only one of those is likely to be destructive. Some of the tsunamis that strike will only affect the general area where they originate while others may travel great distances in several directions, wiping out many cities and villages that are thousands of miles away from each other. It's hard to predict when a tsunami will occur and how strong it will be.

The word "tsunami" translates as "harbor wave" in Japanese. It is a combination of the Japanese word "tsu," which means "harbor," and "nami," which means "wave." Scientists may also refer to a tsunami as a "sea wave." A tsunami is a series of waves created by disturbances in a large body of water. The waves can be high – sometimes as high 70 or 80 feet! That's taller than many buildings! And while tides have nothing to do with the formation of tsunamis, if the tide is high when a tsunami forms, the tsunami may be more severe.

Tsunamis have the potential to cause a considerable amount of destruction in a short amount of time – a tsunami can kill tens of thousands of people in as little as 15 minutes! In light of this, scientists are always trying to learn more about these natural disasters in the hopes of creating accurate early warning systems in an effort to keep people safe.

Let's take a closer look at tsunamis and see what scientists have learned about them over the years.

Chapter 1: What is a Tsunami?

First of all, what is a tsunami? We know now that it is a wave, or series of wave, but what does it look like? What does it sound like? How and when does it form?

Technically, tsunamis are "seismic sea waves," which means that they are generated by the sudden displacement of water in the sea. The most common cause for the formation of a tsunami is the sudden displacement of the actual seafloor, which can occur due to natural disasters, such as earthquakes or landslides.

What does a tsunami look like? A tsunami does not look like the waves you might see at the beach. The waves of a tsunami do not break or curl. As a tsunami approaches the shore, it may appear to looking like a rapidly rising tide, or a series of breaking waves. The water approaches in rapid floods of water. Very violent tsunamis may appear as "bores," which are large, steep waves that look like a step-like wall of water. This kind of tsunami may have a churning, breaking front. Bores form when a tsunami moves rapidly from deep to shallow water.

Tsunami waves hitting shore.
Photo credit: FEMA

The water in a tsunami is usually brown in color, and the wave can reach up to 30 feet or more. It is high enough to crash down on coastal towns and the people who live in them. Viewed from the side, a tsunami resembles most waves you might see in the ocean – it may look like the letter "S" lying longwise. Viewed from above, a tsunami wave resembles a bull's-eye pattern of waves that spread out from a central point or groups of waves that are parallel that move in opposite directions. People who have witnessed a tsunami's approach describe it as looking like a great wall of water – ominous and high – coming at the shore.

Tsunamis look like a giant wave of water when they hit land.

The shape and height of a tsunami is determined by the shape of the ocean floor and the coastline where it strikes. Offshore reefs, which are strips of sand, rocks, or coral that rise from the ocean floor to the surface of the water, may break the force of a tsunami in some areas. Deep valleys, or cracks, in the seafloor may prevent tsunamis from growing too tall.

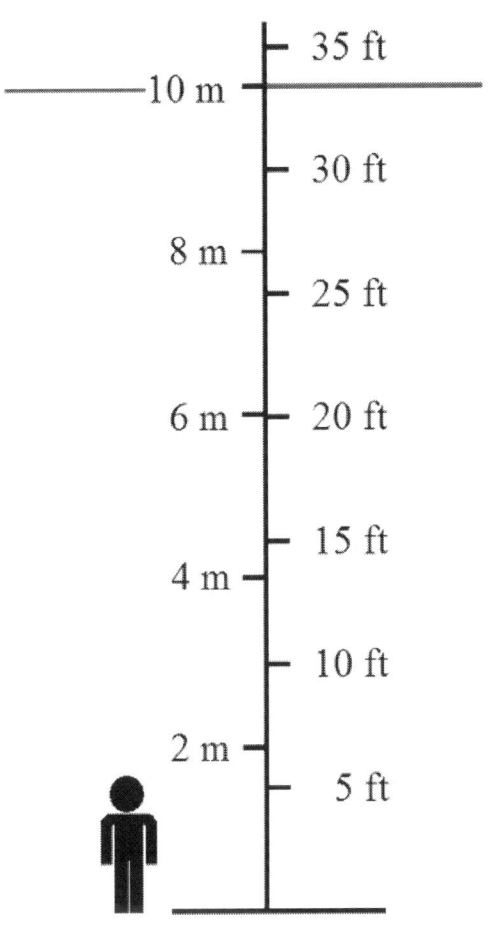

Tsunami size scale.

Survivors of tsunamis often describe the sound of them as they approach land being like a freight train. The sound of a tsunami's approach has also been likened to that of a jet airplane. It is a furious loud whoosh of a sound.

Tsunamis move extremely fast. They can travel at speeds of up to 700 miles per hour (805 km/hr) and can travel from one side of the Pacific Ocean to the other side in less than a day. Regular ocean waves generally only travel, at their fastest, about 50 miles per hour. Even though tsunami waves slow down when they hit the shore, due to the friction caused by the surface of the earth, they still travel approximately 40 miles an hour on land, which is why a human cannot outrun a tsunami wave. Although some people can run as fast as 30 miles an hour, most humans can only run between 5 to 15 miles an hour. This just isn't fast enough to outrun a tsunami!

When tsunami waves are in deep water, they measure less than three feet (.9 m) in height, but they can have lengths as great as 100 miles (161 km) from crest to crest (the "crest" of a wave is its highest part). When these masses of water surge to the surface, the waves spread, moving outward. While this can cause mass destruction when the waves reach land, the same event in the open ocean may go undetected. Because of this, tsunamis can be stealthy at sea. Waves that are capable of causing great destruction on land may pass more or less unnoticed in the open sea. They can even pass under a ship undetected!

By the time a tsunami wave strikes land, it has grown in height. The wave's height is known as its "amplitude." When a tsunami's waves have an amplitude of 130 or more, the occurrence is known as a "megatsunami." The strength and height of a tsunami depends on many factors, such as the shape of the ocean floor and the depth of the water. It depends on the amount and movement of the energy and force that caused it.

While the term "tidal wave" is often used to describe a destructive wall of water, it is not an accurate term for a tsunami. "Tides" are a natural occurrence, caused by the rising and lowering of ocean levels near the shoreline. These are caused by the gravitational pull of the moon. Tsunamis, on the other hand, are caused by violent actions in the earth, such as earthquakes, landslides, or volcanoes. A large meteorite landing in the ocean could also cause a tsunami. When the violent action of the earth displaces water in the ocean, tsunami waves form.

Now that we've established that tsunamis are technically waves and not tides, let's take a closer look at what a wave is, since this information will help us to better understand tsunamis, especially when we examine how the two differ from one another.

Waves

A "wave" is created when energy travels through the water. As it travels, it picks of water particles. The water particles move in circles as the energy of the wave passes through them.

All waves are comprised of parts. These include the "crest," which is the highest point of a wave, and the "trough," which is the lowest point of the wave. The distance from one crest to the next is the "wavelength." The time between one crest passing a point and the next crest passing the same point is called the "wave period." While an average ocean wave has a wavelength of approximately 500 feet (150 m) and a period of 10 seconds, tsunamis have long wavelengths and periods. The wavelength of a tsunami can be as long as 200 miles (322 km) and the period can be up to one hour.

How else do average ocean waves and tsunami waves differ? First of all, while most ocean waves are close to the surface of the ocean, a tsunami wave is different because it stretches all the way down to the ocean's floor in depth and for many miles in width. Most of the waves we see moving ocean water may look powerful, but they affect only the surface of the ocean, not the whole "water column" (which from the surface of the ocean down to the seafloor). Even when water on the surface is rough and choppy, the water in the ocean's depths is calm. But tsunami waves extend all the way down to the floor of the ocean and affect the entire water column.

Additionally, while average ocean waves slow and break as they near the shore, causing the front of the wave to become steeper than the back, tsunamis do not break. And while average ocean waves have white-foam crests at the top when they break, since tsunamis do not break, they generally do not have white crests.

We've noted that tsunamis and tidal waves are not the same thing. "Tidal wave" is a term used to define the rising and ebb of the ocean's levels. This happens gradually, over an extended period of time. You may have seen this if you have visited a beach. You may have noticed the water creeping up further and further on the sand, or, conversely, ebbing away more and more, revealing more sand. It is a steady cycle: the ocean level gets to its highest point (it rises) and then it ebbs away again (it lowers). This happens over and over again, regardless of the season or weather.

This rise and fall of the ocean is a series of long waves called "tides." They are so long they stretch from one side of the earth to the other. The interval of time between the highest tides and the lowest tides is approximately 12 hours. Tides are created by the pull of gravity between the Moon, the Earth, and the Sun. The Moon and the Sun pull on the ocean, causing the entire water body to rise and fall in a predictable manner. Tides are not like ocean waves; they rise and fall gradually, and they never crash onto a beach.

A tsunami wave is not dependent on the weather or the gravitational pull of the Earth, Moon, and Sun. A tsunami wave is a series of waves that only forms when there is a sudden and immense shift of the Earth's water due to a violent force.

The series of waves that makes up a tsunami is known as a "tsunami wave train." There are often no less than ten waves in a tsunami. Tsunamis waves have large distances between the individual crests of the waves. They move like other waves across the ocean, but they are different from other waves, because they have irregular wave train patterns that differ from normal ocean waves. While normal ocean waves have a more consistent wave train pattern, the wave train of a tsunami varies. Some tsunamis have a high initial peak followed by increasingly smaller waves, while others have the highest peak after a series of smaller waves. The reasons for this are dependent on the origin of the tsunami. For instance, a tsunami created by an impact to the water, which causes a sudden displacement, such as the impact of a meteorite, will result in an initial high peak wave. A tsunami created by an event such as an undersea volcanic explosion will have a series of smaller waves gradually increasing to larger waves. The wave train pattern is entirely dependent on the event that caused the tsunami.

Chapter 2: Science of Tsunami's

When an earthquake causes a tsunami, such as in the case of the 2004 south Asia tsunami, it is because two plates of the earth's crust grind together. In this case, it was the Burma plate and the Indian plate. These two particular plates are always grinding against one another. The Indian plate actually pulls the Burma plate down to a small degree, approximately 2.4 inches, every year. But on December 29, 2004, the stress that had built up on the Burma plate cause it to snap. It moved upwards, creating a split more than 600 miles (966 km) long. Some areas of the ocean floor were forced up as much as 50 feet (15 m). This sudden and immense movement displaced many gallons of water in the process, which then generates a tsunami. We will examine this process in closer detail in the following sections.

Causes

As we noted, tsunamis form when there is a sudden and violent displacement of water in the ocean. While earthquakes are the leading source of tsunamis, they can also be caused by volcanic eruptions and underwater events, such as landslides or nuclear explosions. Impact from outer space objects, such as asteroids, may sometimes cause tsunamis, but this is rare.

Plate Tectonics/Earthquakes

The violent action of an earthquake is the most common source of a tsunami. Earthquakes are caused by a sudden movement in "tectonic plates," which are the large plates of rock that form the earth's crust. These plates are what make up the ocean floor and the continents. They are rigid and do not break, bend or deform when they move, except along their edges. The plates move slowly – generally only about 1 to 2 inches (2.5 to 5.1 cm) a year. Occasionally, however, the force of one tectonic plate against another may cause greater movement. This sudden movement is what causes an earthquake.

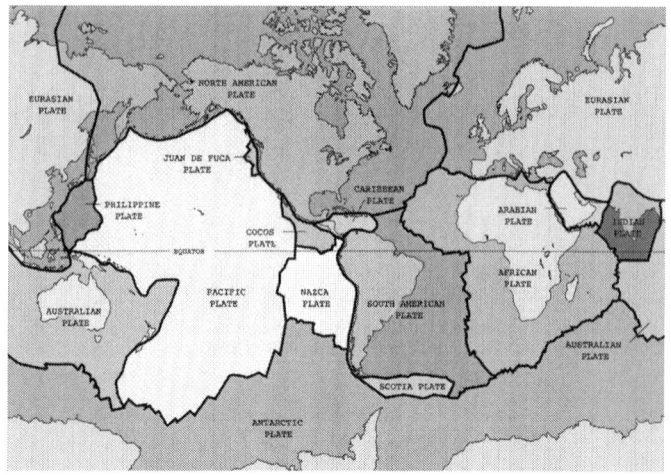

Tectonic plates.
Image credit: U.S. Geological Survey

To understand how this happens, it helps to look at the different types of tectonic plates. There are three types of tectonic plates. "Transform" plates are two plates that slide alongside each other, without moving away or toward one another. "Divergent" plates are plates that are slowly moving away from each other. "Convergent" plates, which move toward each other, are the type of plates may cause an earthquake. When convergent plates move toward each other, one plate may be forced under another. When this happens, it creates a "fault" (a crack in the Earth's crust). If one side of the fault slips to shift up or down suddenly, it causes an earthquake (a series of violent vibrations in the Earth's crust). When this happens, it can result in a sudden displacement of water in the ocean, which in turn can cause a tsunami.

While earthquakes every day, only a few move the ocean floor enough to create waves. This type of earthquake is generally powerful, measuring a 7.5 or higher on the Richter scale. An average of 20 earthquakes in this range occurs each year. Of these, only one or two of these may measure a magnitude of 8 or higher on the Richter scale. The rest of the earthquakes that occur either take place on land or are too far below the ocean floor to create a powerful enough disturbance to cause a tsunami.

Landslides

Landslides are the second most-common cause of tsunamis. A landslide happens when huge pieces of land fall into the water. This sometimes happens during earthquakes. The chunk of land may displace the water and create a tsunami when it falls into the water. This may not only occur when parts of land break off and fall in to the ocean, it may also occur when parts of land that are below the surface of the ocean breaks loose and slides deeper into the water. As it falls, the land pushes water ahead of it and sucks down the water that is behind it.

When a large mass of rock, sand, or mud falls into the ocean, it may create a tsunami if it moves fast enough. This is what happened with the tsunami that struck Lituya Bay in southeastern Alaska in 1958. An earthquake registering 8.0 on the Richter scale shook the area and caused part of a mountain to slide into the water, which in turn caused a tsunami.

Some storms may be capable of causing a submarine landslide that may result in a tsunami even if the storm waves do not reach the seafloor. This is because large storms can create a "storm surge," a mound of water in front of the storm that can reach heights of 20-32 feet (6-10 m). As the storm surge moves onto land, it is frequently preceded by a drop in air pressure, which may cause pressure changes on the seafloor. This is what may create a tsunami. An example of this is the tsunami event that happened in Japan in 1923. On September 1st, a typhoon raged across Tokyo, Japan, which was followed by a submarine landslide and earthquake that created a 36-foot (11 m) high tsunami that killed 143,000 in Tokyo.

The characteristic of tsunamis created by landslides depend on several factors, including the amount of material that moves during the landslide, the depth the material moves to, and the speed at which it moves.

Volcanoes

Volcanoes can also cause tsunamis. During the past 250 years, volcanoes caused approximately 90 tsunamis.

A volcano is an opening in the Earth's crust through which magma, the hot, liquid rock that is beneath the surface of the earth, and hot gases can escape. When the pressure of the gases and magma builds and forces through the opening, an eruption occurs. If the eruption happens underwater and is violent, it can release a lot of energy and create "shock waves," which can cause a tsunami to form. Some of the largest recorded tsunamis have been caused by volcanic eruptions.

Volcanoes can cause tsunamis when they erupt and send massive amounts of lava and rock into the ocean, either by direct flow or by falling into the ocean after flying through the sky. Approximately 20 percent of volcano-induced tsunamis happen when volcanic ash or pyroclastic flow (a dense, destructive mass of intensely hot ash, lava fragments, and gases ejected explosively from a volcano and typically flowing at great speeds) hit the ocean, displacing large amounts of water. An example of a tsunami caused by a volcanic eruption is the tsunami that happened in 1883 when the volcano at Krakatau erupted and formed a 130-foot (40 m) high tsunami that killed approximately 36, 500 people.

Volcanoes can also create tsunamis indirectly. For instance, when hot lava comes into contact with ocean water it may cause it to heat up so quickly that the water expands and creates a tsunami wave. Another way a volcano can cause a tsunami is to collapse and fall into itself after erupting. The water above it and around it may get sucked downward during the collapse, causing waves due to the sudden displacement.

Meteorites

Tsunamis can result when a meteorite, a large piece of rock from space that enters the Earth's atmosphere, strikes the surface of the ocean. It the meteorite is large enough, the force of the impact can create a tsunami. Although such an event has never been witnessed, scientists speculate that a meteorite may have struck the Earth and created a tsunami as recently as 3.5 billion years ago. Geologists also estimate that approximately 65 million years ago, an asteroid or comet plunged into the shallow sea in the area that is currently known as the Yucatan Peninsula in Mexico. The asteroid or comet is estimated to have been more than 6 miles (10 km) in diameter. When it struck the water, it created a "megatsunami" (a tsunami that has enough energy to travel to coastlines in many parts of the world) that spread around the world. It waves, estimated to be 150 to 300 feet (50 to 100 km) flooded the areas that are currently the southern states of the U.S. and Mexico. Geologists are able to make these estimates based on the evidence the tsunami left in its wake, including thick layers of rock composed of mud, sand, and broken rock fragments.

While this was a large object from space that fell into the ocean, even a smaller extraterrestrial object could create a significant tsunami wave that would result in flooding and damage.

Chapter 3: Where Tsunamis Strike

Most tsunamis occur along the shores of the Pacific Ocean. The areas that are at the highest risk for tsunamis include the coastal areas of Japan, the Phillipines, and the American west coast and Hawaii. The Pacific Ocean is the world's largest ocean, covering more than one third of the total surface area of our planet. The area that surrounds the Pacific Ocean is called "the Ring of Fire," which consists of many mountain chains and deep ocean trenches and is about 40,000km long. It runs from the tip of South America, up the coast of Chile, Peru, and Ecuador, through Central America and the west coast of Mexico, the United States and Canada. It extends to all the way to the southern coast of Alaska and along the Aleutian Islands, and then follows along the coast of Japan and the Philippines. It ends in New Zealand. Tsunamis may form anywhere along this horseshoe shaped rim.

Why is the Ring of Fire more likely to have tsunamis than other areas? The reason is because the area has more seismic and volcanic activity than other areas. Several of the Earth's tectonic plates push against each other in this region, creating ideal conditions for earthquakes and volcanic activity. Because of this, the Ring of Fire has 90% of the world's earthquakes and 75% of its volcanoes. Although approximately four out of every five tsunamis happen in this area, they also frequently occur in other areas, such as the Indian Ocean and the Mediterranean Sea.

The first places to be hit in the case of a tsunami caused by an earthquake are the towns and areas in close proximity to the earthquake's epicenter. A strong tsunami will be able to travel vast distances and strike areas far away from where it originates. For instance, the 2004 Indian Ocean tsunami first struck the communities near its epicenter in Sumatra and other nearby islands and then hit places further away, including India and Africa. Remember, a tsunami can travel fast – up to 700 miles per hour (805 km/hr) – and can travel across the Pacific Ocean in less than a day.

Development

As we have seen, the first thing that happens in the development of a tsunami is that a seismic event, such as an earthquake, occurs and sends "shock waves" outward. The initial waves of the tsunami are only a few feet high and travel fast. As the waves approach the coast, they travel through water that is shallower than it is further out at sea, and this causes the waves to decrease in speed while they are, at the same time, increasing in height. Keep in mind that as the wave slows down and increases in height, it is not losing any energy. While the waves display a reduction in wavelength, their frequency (the number of waves that pass a fixed point in unit time) remains constant. This process is known as the "shoaling" effect. By the time they strike the coast, the height of the waves combined with their frequency causes them to hit with deadly force. Tsunamis that strike the shore near the epicenter of an earthquake can reach heights of 100 feet (30 m) or more.

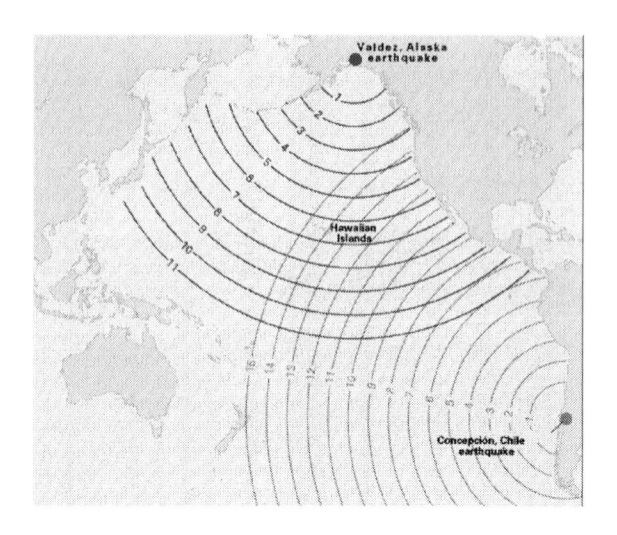

Travel times (in hours) are shown for the tsunamis produced by the 1960 Concepción, Chile, earthquake (purple curves) and by the 1964 Good Friday, Valdez (Anchorage), Alaska earthquake (red curves).

Image Credit: U.S. Geological Survey

The speed of a tsunami depends on gravity and the depth of the water. The deeper the water, the faster the wave. As the waves move into shallow water, they slow down. Since a single tsunami wave can be long, its front portion can be in shallow water while its rear portion is still in deep water. This means that the rear portion will move faster than the front portion. When this happens, the waves bunch up and get higher as the rear portion catches up to the front portion. Because the wave does not lose much energy as it moves onto land, this effect can cause a powerful tsunami, since the energy becomes concentrated in less water with higher waves.

Kinds of Tsunamis—Distant and Local

There are two kinds of tsunamis. "Distant" tsunamis are those that are created more than 600 miles (966 km) offshore. They are far enough away from land so that people have enough time to get to higher ground before they strike because scientists can predict them easier and give adequate warning. "Local" tsunamis, on the other hand, are much more dangerous. They are created somewhere between 60 miles (97 km) and 600 miles (988 km) from shore. They hit land within a very short time after forming – often within minutes. Because there is not enough time for a warning to be issued, these are the tsunamis that may take many lives. While landslides are often the cause of local tsunamis, they can also be caused by earthquakes. In some cases, a tsunami can be both distant and local. For instance, the Indian Ocean tsunami that occurred in 2004 was a local tsunami for communities in Sumatra and other nearby islands, but it was a distant tsunami for places farther away, such as India and Africa.

Another example of a distant tsunami is the powerful wave that was created when an earthquake shot through the ocean floor near the Kamchatka Peninsula of Russia in November, 1952. The resulting tsunami wave traveled across the Pacific Ocean and hit Japan, Hong Kong, Micronesia, Papua New Guinea, Kiribati, the Solomon Islands, Mexico, Guatemala, El Salvador, Costa Rica, Nicaragua, Ecuador, Chile, Peru, British Columbia, Washington, Alaska, Oregon, California, Hawaii, and New Zealand, all within a day!

Prediction

At the Pacific Tsunami Warning Center in Hawaii, scientists use seismometers to detect disturbances in the Earth's seismic activity. A seismometer records the movements of the earth, which can be used to detect earthquakes and measure their strength. It does this by detecting rumblings within the earth and measuring the vibrations inside of the Earth's crust. It then rates these vibrations on the Richter scale (a numerical scale that expresses the magnitude of an earthquake based on seismograph oscillations with values that fall between 0 and 9). Using these observations, scientists can foretell a tsunami, since tsunamis are often caused by earthquakes. For instance, when a tsunami hit the coastal towns in Indonesia, Sri Lanka, Thailand, and India on December 26, 2004, the center detected the earthquake that caused it in the Indian Ocean. It quickly sent out a warning of the possibility of a tsunami near the epicenter (the central point) of the earthquake. At first, they thought the earthquake was a magnitude 8.0 earthquake, which is strong but not catastrophic. But as more data emerged, they realized it was a serious earthquake. It turned out to be the most powerful earthquake the world had seen in over forty years! It measured 9.0 on the Richter scale, the highest value that can be assigned.

Scientists also use a combination of bottom pressure recorders and floating buoys to help predict tsunamis. A bottom pressure recorder is a device that measures the change in height of the water column by measuring associated changes in the water pressure. It measures the water pressure in the ocean every 15 minutes. By doing so, it can help to detect the passage of a tsunami since the pressure of the water on the seafloor is directly related to the sea-surface height. If the bottom pressure recorder picks up unusual activity, it will begin to measure the water pressure every 15 seconds to obtain more information.

Floating buoys are also an important tool that is used to help predict tsunamis. They work is combination with bottom pressure recorders. Floating buoys measure the conditions on the surface of the deep sea and send that data, as well as the data received via an acoustic link from the bottom pressure recorder, to a satellite. After the information is sent to the satellite, it will be transmitted to scientists at watch centers around the world. This system is known as DART (Deep-ocean Assessment and Reporting of Tsunamis) and plays a critical role in helping scientists to predict tsunamis.

DART surface buoy.

Sea level and tide gauges, which measure the sea level and tides at the shoreline, are also used to detect tsunamis. While they are primarily used for monitoring the tides for navigational purposes, tsunami warning centers also depend upon this data to observe the sea level and to determine whether tsunamis may have been generated during an earthquake. The gauges are located on piers in harbors along coastlines worldwide and send data in real time to tsunami watch centers. Many of these gauges use solar panels so that they will function even in the event of a power outage.

Other methods scientists use to guess where tsunamis may occur in the future include using historical records and generating computer programs to predict tsunamis. By looking at historical patterns of tsunami occurrence, for instance, scientists can create a database that may aid in predicting when in where tsunamis may occur in the future. Likewise, in the event of an earthquake, state-of-the-art computer programs can help to predict how long a tsunami triggered by the earthquake would take to reach places near its epicenter and beyond, even though there is not yet evidence a wave exists. This could help to provide accurate information to officials who may have only a few minutes in which to decide whether or not to sound an alarm. These sorts of computer-generated tools can be invaluable to scientists who are trying to forecast and predict when and where a tsunami might strike.

Chapter 4: Warning Signs

Some of the earliest warning signs can be observed and should be noted. Receding waters, for example, are a strong warning sign of the possibility of a tsunami. The water goes far out to sea, leaving a bare and naked beach behind. Many people may be deceived by this, and may even "play" on the beach that is bared as the ocean's waters recede, marveling at the pretty fish that are stranded and at the shells and other sea life left behind. They may try to "save" the fish and other sea life stranded on the rocks. Unbeknownst to them, however, the ocean's water has only briefly receded. It is about to return with a vengeance! The tides that have receded will soon come back in great quantity, and they will come back quickly. The best thing to do when you observe ocean water rapidly recede is to move to higher ground to a safe place as soon as possible.

When the water level along a seacoast rapidly drops like this suddenly right before a tsunami hits, it is known as a "drawback." It occurs rapidly and is caused by the valleys in between the waves of the tsunami. How does this happen? The best way to understand it is to consider that all waves have a "ridge" (which is high) and a "trough" (which is low). Either of these may be the first to arrive when a tsunami strikes. If the first part to hit is the ridge, observers will see a massive wave approaching. However, if the first part of the wave to strike is the "trough," the shoreline will recede and expose areas that are usually underwater. The sea will go out, leaving the ocean floor exposed. Fish and boats are stranded on the sand. Many people are curious when this happens and may walk out into the exposed sand to explore. But, as we've noted, this is an action that could cost them their life – soon after the waters drawback, the first wave of the tsunami will hit.

How much time does a person have to evacuate the area when a drawback occurs? To calculate this, consider that a typical wave period (or frequency) for a tsunami wave is approximately 12 minutes. This means that, during the drawback phase, the areas below sea level will be exposed after 3 minutes. Then, during the next 6 minutes, the trough will refill. In the next 6 minutes, the wave will change from a ridge to a trough again, causing the waters to drain again. This second drawback may sweep people who are on the exposed beach and debris out to sea. The process repeats when the next wave arrives.

What are other warning signs that a tsunami is about to happen? Some people theorize that animals can tell when a tsunami or earthquake is forming by sensing the geological changes in the earth. When a tsunami strikes, few animals seem to be caught off guard. There have been several reported instances of animals making their way to higher ground in the moments before a tsunami hits. For instance, witnesses reported elephants screaming and running for higher ground and flamingos abandoning their low-lying breeding ground just before the Indian Ocean tsunami made landfall. Dogs refused to go indoors, and zoo animals rushed into their shelters and would not come out. Experts suggest that the acute hearing and other senses animals have might make it possible for them to hear or feel the Earth's vibration and react. Very few animals die during tsunamis. They all make their way to higher ground.

Warning Systems

It is important to first distinguish the difference between a "Tsunami Watch" and a "Tsunami Warning." A "tsunami watch" means that there is a possibility of a tsunami and that people should be alert. A "tsunami warning" means that an actual tsunami may strike and that the area should be evacuated immediately. The Pacific Tsunami Warning Center automatically issues a Tsunami Watch for any earthquake magnitude 7.5 or larger (7.0 or larger in the Aleutian Islands) if the epicenter is in an area capable of generating a tsunami. They notify Civil Defense and provide the local media with public announcements. They then keep a close eye on tide gauge stations to see if a tsunami has been generated or not.

If the data reported by the stations confirms that a tsunami has been generated, a Tsunami Warning will be issued. A warning may be issued automatically if the system detects an earthquake powerful enough to create a tsunami nearby. The public will be alerted via the emergency broadcast system and evacuation will begin immediately.

Early warning systems, such as the DART (Deep-ocean Assessment and Reporting of Tsunamis) system mentioned earlier as a way of predicting tsunamis, also serves as a warning system for tsunamis. It is utilized by the Pacific Tsunami Warning Center system set up in the Pacific Ocean basin. Operated by the United States, this system allows for real-time tsunami detection to be made as waves travel across open ocean waters. It relies on buoys and equipment that measures water displacement and the pressure of sea waves to detect tsunamis. The equipment is highly sensitive to changes in vibrations in the earth and can alert people who live along the coasts of approaching tsunamis. After the data is transmitted via satellite to scientists, they will use it to warn the public via radio, television and sirens.

The Pacific Tsunami Warning Center was the first warning system to be put in place, but other similar warning systems now exist around the world, including The International Tsunami Warning System, which serves countries in or along the Pacific Ocean, including Australia, Canada, Chile, China, Guatemala, Indonesia, Japan, Mexico, the Philippines, and the United States, and the Japanese Tsunami Warning Service, which serves Japan.

While there was no warning system in place in the Indian Ocean before the tsunami struck in 2004, steps have since been taken since to establish one. The system is engineered to provide warning of approaching tsunamis to inhabitants of nations bordering the Indian Ocean. It includes a network of local communications that will help to spread warnings of approaching tsunamis (25 seismographic stations relaying information to 26 national tsunami information centers) and a monitoring system comprised of three deep-ocean sensors for predicting the possibility of a tsunami. The system became active in late June 2006.

The system was activated April 11, 2012 after a strong earthquake occurred off the west coast of Sumatra in Indonesia. It performed well overall during this first ocean-wide test, according to the Intergovernmental Oceanographic Commission of the United Nations Educational, Scientific and Cultural Organization (UNESC).

Chapter 5:Richter Scale

The Richter magnitude scale, frequently referred to as simply the Richter scale, was developed to as a mathematical device to compare the size of earthquakes and assign a single number to measure the energy released during an earthquake. It is used to measure the strength, or "magnitude," of earthquakes. The Richter scale is a "logarithmic" scale, which means that each step on it is about 10 times stronger than the one before it. For example, an earthquake measuring 5.0 is ten times greater in strength than an earthquake measuring 4.0.

The Richter scale was developed in 1935 by Charles Francis Richter at the California Institute of Technology. Although it was first intended for use only in a particular study area in California, it eventually became the standard tool used to measure earthquake magnitude worldwide. Scientists sue the Richter scale to determine whether an earthquake is strong enough to generate a tsunami.

Damage

A tsunami is devastating when it strikes – it can crush buildings, sweep away cars, and snap trees and utility poles in half. When a tsunami strikes, it sweeps away everything in it path. A tsunami's destructive power comes from its towering heights. The fast-moving massive wall of water can cause great destruction. It can sweep away entire towns and villages. Many of the people who survive a tsunami are left without homes to return to.

Debris left behind after tsunami.
Photo credit: U.S. Navy photo by Mass Communication Specialist 3rd Class Alexander Tidd

A tsunami can also take many lives. The tsunami that struck the coastal towns on the Indian Ocean in 2004 claimed 220, 000 lives. Tens of thousands of people were injured. The flooding that results may kill people, or they may be struck by debris during the flood. Tsunamis can travel up rivers and cause flooding far inland. The places that are in the most danger of being destroyed are those within 1 mile (1.6 km) of the shore and 50 feet (15 m) above sea level. The debris that travels in the flood can move at great speeds, killing or injuring those in its path.

As you can see, a tsunami can be one of the worst of natural disasters. The sheer power of the water in a tsunami wave is tremendous. Consider that a cubic foot of seawater weighs 64 pounds. There are millions of cubic feet of seawater in a tsunami wave! Additionally, the fast-moving waves behind the first wave of a tsunami catch up to it as it nears land and is slowed by friction. These waves add to the force and height of the first wave. But the first wave of a tsunami is not always the most powerful. Sometimes the waves behind it have just as much power, or more.

Tsunamis can also do other damage besides flooding. They can also spark fires when they hit land by splitting open containers filled with flammable liquids and gases, such as gasoline or oil. Oil-slicked ocean water in the tsunami can cause the flames to spread.

Tsunamis also often cause massive erosion – a process where water moves rock and dirt away from the ocean coast that normally takes place over a long period of time – in a brief period of time. A tsunami can strip a beach of its sand, and wash away soil and plants on the coastline. Damage to coastal cities and towns can be minimized by building sturdy sea walls and planting vegetation in the shallow waters along the shore.

Japanese coastline after withdrawal of tsunami.

Photo credit: NOAA/NGDC, Takaaki Uda, Public Works Research Institute, Japan.

Cleaning Up

After a tsunami strikes, there is much work to do in its aftermath. Organizations from around the world join together to do the immediate work of reuniting families, setting up temporary housing for those whose homes were destroyed in the tsunami, providing food and water, tending to the injured, and removing the dead. In the days and weeks following a tsunami, the main focus is on helping people to re-establish their lives after the disaster.

A Japanese search and rescue team searches the rubble near a high-rise building in Japan.
Photo credit: U.S. Navy photo by Mass Communication Specialist 3rd Class Alexander Tidd

After the dead have been buried and a daily routine has been put into place for the survivors, there is still much work to do. Entire communities must be rebuilt. This process can take several months, even years. Two years after a magnitude 9.0 earthquake struck Japan and generated a tsunami on March 11, 2011, work was still underway to rebuild the areas that were affected by it.

Chapter 6: Famous Tsunamis

8 Deadliest Tsunamis

1. Indian Ocean, 2004 (225,000 + deaths).
2. Crete-Santorini, Ancient Greece, 1410 B.C. (100,000 deaths).
3. Portugal-Morocco, 1755 (60,000 deaths).
4. South Sea China, 1782 (40,000 deaths)
5. Krakatau, Indonesia, 1883 (36,500 deaths).
6. Tokaido-Nankaido, Japan, 1707 (30,000 deaths).
7. Sanriku, Japan, 1896 (26, 360 deaths).
8. Northern Chile, 1868 (25, 674 deaths).

Notable Tsunamis in History

When the **Krakatoa** volcano, located in Southeast Asia on the Indonesian island of Rakata, erupted in **1883**, it birthed four tsunamis that spread and crashed into the shores of Java and Sumatra, located in the Sunda Strait. The waves reached heights of 131 feet (40 m) and killed approximately 40,000 people.

On April 1, 1946, a magnitude 7.8 earthquake struck the **Aleutian Islands** in Alaska. Five hours later, the tsunami this created hit Hilo, Hawaii. 159 people were killed, and the town was destroyed.

In 1958, an earthquake registering 8.0 on the Richter scale shook **Lituya Bay**, located in southeastern Alaska. The earthquake caused part of a mountain to slide into the water, which caused a tsunami. When the wave reached the opposite shore, it produced a water surge measuring 1, 722 feet (525 m), making it the largest tsunami ever recorded. Everything in the wave's path was stripped off of the mountain, leaving a barren area that can still be seen today.

On May 22, 1960, a magnitude 9.5 earthquake occurred off the coast of **Chile, South America**. It was the largest earthquake ever recorded. It created a series of deadly waves that spread across the Pacific Ocean. Within 15 minutes of the earthquake, walls of water hit along the coast of Chile, killing approximately 5,000 people. Fifteen hours later, the tsunami reached the Hawaiian Islands. Hardest hit was the Hawaiian city of Hilo. Its waterfront area was destroyed, and 61 people were killed. The tsunami hit Japan twenty-two hours later with a 20-foot (6 m) wave, killing approximately 200 people.

People run from an approaching tsunami in Hilo, Hawaii on 1 April 1946.

Image credit: Pacific Tsunami Museum in Hilo, Hawaii

On March 27, 1964, the strongest earthquake to ever occur in North America happened in **southern Alaska**, about 75 miles (121 km) east of Anchorage, Alaska. It was a 9.2 magnitude earthquake. It shook the ground in downtown Anchorage for a full five minutes. The earthquake killed nine people. It created a massive tsunami, the most destructive to ever strike the west coast of the United States and Canada. It killed 106 people in Alaska, 4 in Oregon, and 11 in Crescent City, California. The wave was at a height of 220 feet (67 m) when it struck the Valdez Inlet in Alaska and had declined to 21 feet (6.4 m) by the time it hit California. The tsunami moved along the coast at a speed of 500 miles per hour (805 km/hr).

Aftermath of Alaska 1964 tsunami.
Photo credit: NOAA

On July 17, 1998, an underwater earthquake in the southwestern Pacific near **Papua New Guiana** caused a tsunami. Approximately 2, 202 people were killed.

On December 26, 2004, a tsunami in the **Indian Ocean** hit the coast of South Asia, killing more than 220,000 people. The tsunami hit more than 11 countries in the region, including Thailand, Malaysia, Indonesia, Burma, Sri Lanka, India and Somalia. Waves even hit Africa, which is about 3,000 miles (4,828 km) away from the origin of the tsunami. The hardest hit area was the northwestern tip of the Indonesian island of Sumatra. The epicenter of the earthquake that caused the tsunami was only 150 miles (241 km) offshore of the island, and about 18 miles (29 km) below the surface of the ocean. Lasting almost a full nine minutes, the earthquake that caused the tsunami was the third most powerful earthquake ever measured. The earthquake that caused the Indian Ocean tsunami of 2004 measured 9.0 on the Richter scale. It was the most powerful earthquake in over 40 years. It ruptured a section of the ocean crust 750 miles (1,200 km) long and 60 miles (100 km) wide. It moved rocks approximately 50 feet (15 m) in as little as three minutes.

Chapter 7: Studying

Scientists study tsunamis to try to figure out where and how they started. This not only helps them to predict and warn people about where the current waves may travel, it also provides insights into ways to predict tsunamis in the future. They use a variety of tools to study tsunamis, including computers, seismographs, and models, such as the SWASH (Simulating Waves until at Shore) model, used to calculate how tall a wave is, how fast it's moving, and how much energy it holds.

Scientists study a variety of aspects of tsunamis in an effort to learn more about them so changes can be made that may help to save lives. They do this by compiling the data they collect to help understand and predict tsunami events and where and how they might strike. For instance, they may study the shape of the ocean floor and the coastlines and put the information into a computer so that they can predict how tall a tsunami in the area might be and what part of the coastline is vulnerable to flooding. In doing this, scientists can predict with fair accuracy which areas are likely to be the worst hit during a tsunami and steps can be taken to put practices into place that promote public safety. For example, "tsunami evacuation zones" can be created in places that are vulnerable and laws can be established that forbid building structures in the areas prone to damage from tsunamis.

Safety

If you are in an area where there is a high risk for a tsunami, some steps can be taken to help keep you safe in the event of a tsunami. Above all, be aware of how high above sea level you are, whether you live in the area or are visiting. Figure out how far away you are from the coast. Make a plan to get to higher ground in case of a tsunami warning. Make sure everyone in your family knows what the plan is. Keep emergency supplies on hand and have them in a place where you can get to them quickly. These should include a flashlight, batteries, a first-aid kit, a battery-operated radio, necessary prescription medications, blankets, and food and water.

When a *tsunami watch* has been issued, stay away from the beach. Watch and listen to the weather radio or news for more information. When a *tsunami warning* has been issued, move to higher ground immediately, taking your emergency supplies with you. Move quickly. Just a matter of moments can save lives.

Conclusion

While tsunamis carry potential for devastating destruction, many factors can reduce the damage, particularly awareness and preparation as well as education and research. Understanding how tsunamis form and develop and knowing what steps to take when one strikes can minimize the damage that may result from these natural disasters. Advancements in early warning systems in recent years have made a critical difference in helping to save lives in the future.

Bibliography

Australian Government Bureau of Meteorology. "Tsunami Facts and Information." http://www.bom.gov.au/tsunami/info/

Fine, Jill. Tsunamis. Children's Press: New York. 2007.

Fradin, Judy and Dennis. *Tsunamis: Witness to Disaster.* National Geographic: Washington, D.C. 2008.

González, Frank I. "Tsunami!" *Scientific American, 280,* 56–65 (1999). http://www.pmel.noaa.gov/pubs/outstand/gonz2088/gonz2088.shtml

Hamilton, John. *Tsunamis.* ABDO Daughters: Edina, Minnesota. 2006

Mott, Maryann. "Did Animals Sense the Tsunami Was Coming?" *National Geographic News*, January 4, 2005. http://news.nationalgeographic.com/news/2005/01/0104_050104_tsunami_animals.html

NOAA brochure. "Tsunami: the Great Waves." http://www.nws.noaa.gov/om/brochures/tsunami2.htm

NOAA Center for Tsunami Research. "DART® (Deep-ocean Assessment and Reporting of Tsunamis." http://nctr.pmel.noaa.gov/Dart/

NOAA's National Weather Service, Pacific Tsunami Warning Center. "Frequently Asked Questions (FAQ)." http://ptwc.weather.gov/faq.php

Oregon Department of Geology and Industries website. "Geologic Hazards on the Oregon Coast The science of tsunamis."
http://www.oregongeology.com/sub/earthquakes/coastal/ScienceofTsunamis.htm

United Nations Educational, Scientific and Cultural Organization (UNESCO): Intergovernmental Oceanographic Commission website. "Indian Ocean Tsunami Warning System performed well, detailed assessment underway." April 13, 2012.
http://www.unesco.org/new/en/natural-sciences/ioc-oceans/single-view-oceans/news/indian_ocean_wide_tsunami_watch/

United States Geological Survey (USGS) Earthquake Hazards Program website. "The Richter Scale."
http://earthquake.usgs.gov/learn/topics/richter.php

University of Hawaii at Hilo's Natural Hazards Big Island website. "Understanding the difference between a tsunami "watch" and "warning."

http://www.uhh.hawaii.edu/~nat_haz/tsunamis/watchvwarning.php

Printed in Great Britain
by Amazon